Success With
Reading Tests

SCHOLASTIC

Editor: Ourania Papacharalambous
Cover design by Tannaz Fassihi; cover illustration by Kevin Zimmer
Interior design by Michelle Kim

ISBN 978-1-338-79867-8
Scholastic Inc., 557 Broadway, New York, NY 10012
Copyright © 2022 Scholastic Inc.
All rights reserved. Printed in the U.S.A.
First printing, January 2022
2 3 4 5 6 7 8 9 10   40   29 28 27 26 25 24 23

INTRODUCTION

The Scholastic Success With Reading Tests series is designed to help you help students succeed on standardized tests. In this workbook for sixth graders, the 10 four-page tests are culled from the reading skills practice tests provided three times a year to *Scholastic News Edition 6* subscribers, with some new and revised material. By familiarizing students with the skills, language, and formats they will encounter on state and national tests, these practice tests will boost confidence and help raise scores.

The Reading Comprehension portion of the tests measures a student's ability to read and understand different types of prose. The tests contain passages of various lengths and about various subjects. Some of the questions require students to form an understanding based on information that is explicitly stated in the passage; others require forming an understanding based on information that is only implicit in the passage.

The questions supporting each test are specifically designed to review the following skills:

o **Find the Main Idea**   o **Understand Vocabulary**

o **Identify Sequence**   o **Recognize Author's Purpose**

o **Read for Detail**   o **Make Inferences**

o **Identify Cause and Effect**   o **Identify Fact and Opinion**

The Vocabulary portion of the tests measures a student's vocabulary and varies with each test. Some tests task students with identifying synonyms and antonyms; others require students to use context to choose a word that best completes a sentence.

Note that the tests in the second half of the book are slightly more difficult. These are designed to be given later in the school year.

In addition to helping students prepare for "real" tests, the practice tests in this workbook may be used as a diagnostic tool, to help you detect individual students' strengths and weaknesses, or as an instructional tool, for oral reading and discussion.

Keep in mind that our practice tests are just that—practice. These tests are not standardized. They should not be used to determine grade level, to compare one student's performance with that of others, or to evaluate teachers' abilities

HOW TO USE AND ADMINISTER THE TESTS

Before administering each test, you may wish to review with students some basic information as well as helpful test-taking strategies, such as reading the questions before reading the passages.

- Establish a relaxed atmosphere. Explain to students that they will not be graded and that they are taking the test to practice for "real" tests down the road.

- Encourage students to do their best, but not to worry if they don't know all the answers.

- Provide each student with a sharpened pencil with a good eraser.

- Review the directions, then read the samples in each section and discuss the answers. Be sure to pay close attention to the directions in the vocabulary section on the last page of each test.

- To mimic the atmosphere of a real test, you may wish to set time limits. Students should be able to complete the reading comprehension section (the first three pages of each test) in 20 to 25 minutes. Allow an additional 10 minutes for the vocabulary portion on the last page of each test. Encourage students to work quickly and carefully and to keep track of the remaining time—just as they would in a real testing session.

- During the test, walk around the room and, as needed, guide students to:
  - make sure that they mark one answer circle for each question.
  - be sure to read the passages before marking answers.
  - use an eraser to make any changes to answers.
  - not copy the work of other students.

- If students are taking too much time with a particular question, tell them to eliminate the answer choices that are wrong first, then to choose the answer they think is the best choice from the remaining answers. (While "guessing" is not to be encouraged, encouraging students to mark an answer, even if they are not sure, will help them make use of whatever partial knowledge they may have.)

- Watch for students who stop working before they have done all the questions and encourage them to keep working.

- Encourage students to check their work after they have finished.

At the back of this book, you will find Tested Skills charts and an Answer Key for the 10 Practice Tests. The Tested Skills charts list the core standards and skills and the test questions that measure each. The charts may be helpful to you in determining what kinds of questions students answered incorrectly, what skills they may be having trouble with, and who may need further instruction in particular skills.

Reading Skills Practice Test 1
Reading Comprehension

Read each passage. Then, fill in the circle that best completes each sentence or answers each question.

SAMPLE

Since 1870, the National Weather Service has been trying to do a very difficult job—predict the weather. Today, this government agency gives out a weather **forecast** four times a day. To make its forecasts, the Weather Service uses information collected from land stations, ships, and weather radars.

1 In this passage the word **forecast** means
(A) warning.
(B) prediction.
(C) sample.
(D) hurricane.

2 What is the best title for this passage?
(A) "Weather Forecasting in 1870"
(B) "You Can't Predict the Weather"
(C) "The National Weather Service"
(D) "Land Stations, Ships, and Weather Radars"

A. Peer **mediation** helps cut down on playground fighting and school suspensions. With peer mediation, kids in grades 4 to 12 are trained to settle arguments before they turn into fights. When a disagreement breaks out, two mediators step in. They listen to both sides and ask students how they want to see the problem resolved. If both kids agree to the terms, the mediators draw up a contract for each to sign. As long as they stick to the agreement, everyone wins!

Peer-mediation programs also boost the mediators' self-esteem. As one mediator said, "I learned I could help people."

1 In this passage the word **mediation** means
(A) resolving conflicts.
(B) writing contracts.
(C) using violence to end arguments.
(D) ignoring conflicts.

2 This passage is mostly about
(A) playground fights.
(B) new playground games.
(C) ways to boost your self-esteem.
(D) peer-mediation programs.

3 What do peer mediators do first?
(A) They draw up a contract.
(B) They listen to each side.
(C) They ask a teacher for help.
(D) They force both kids to agree.

B.   When people think about the countries of Europe, Andorra rarely comes to mind. That's probably because it's so tiny—just 180 square miles in all. It's located on the border of Spain and France, in a mountain range called the Pyrenees.

Andorra became independent in 1993. That year, its 50,000 citizens voted in elections for the very first time. Most Andorrans speak a language called Catalan. Like French and Spanish, Catalan is a Latin-based language.

Visitors come to Andorra to hike or ski in the mountains, and also to shop. Andorra has a low sales tax, so bargain hunters stream in from the neighboring countries. And there's no need to change currency; Andorra uses the Euro.

1   What is the best title for this passage?
   Ⓐ "The World's Tiniest Countries"
   Ⓑ "Andorra, a Mountain Country"
   Ⓒ "The Border of France and Spain"
   Ⓓ "Why You Should Shop in Andorra"

2   From this passage, you might guess that
   Ⓐ France and Spain also have a low sales tax.
   Ⓑ countries should charge sales tax.
   Ⓒ Andorra will soon raise its sales tax.
   Ⓓ both France and Spain probably have a higher sales tax.

3   Most Andorrans speak
   Ⓐ Catalan.   Ⓒ French.
   Ⓑ Latin.   Ⓓ Andorran.

C.   Scientists recently found a 290-million-year-old fossil, or imprint in rock, which they say is proof that an early reptile ran faster than any other living creature at that time—and it did it on two legs! The reptile, less than one foot long, was running around on its two back legs 80 million years before the first known dinosaur did so. This means the newly **discovered** reptile named *Eudibamus cursoris* (you-da-bom-us cur-sor-us) is the first known creature to walk on its two back legs. The reptile likely ran in an upright position, like humans and some dinosaurs. Scientists believe the reptile started running upright so it could escape the hungry meat-eaters that hunted it.

1   What can you conclude is the most important aspect of this fossil discovery?
   Ⓐ The fossil shows the first reptile that moved on its two back legs.
   Ⓑ The fossil is an imprint of a reptile that is found in a rock.
   Ⓒ The fossil is 290 million years old.
   Ⓓ The reptile was less than one foot long.

2   Scientists believe that the reptile started running upright on its two back legs because
   Ⓐ it was sick of going around on four legs.
   Ⓑ it was only one foot long, which was too short to walk on four legs.
   Ⓒ it was trying to escape the hungry meat eaters that hunted it.
   Ⓓ it ran faster than all other creatures.

D. "I want to start a garden," Pablo told Mr. Cordiz, the store owner.

"Very good," Mr. Cordiz replied. "Which kinds of plants do you want to grow? They should be suited to the growing conditions in your backyard. Do you get a lot of sun?"

Pablo nodded his head yes.

Mr. Cordiz pointed to some plants with colorful blooms. "In our area, snapdragons, poppies, and pansies are annuals," he said. "They start and finish their life cycles in one growing season. They will die in late fall. Sometimes they reseed themselves, but most likely next spring, you'll have to buy more and plant them again. These annuals like the sun."

Then, he pointed to some other plants in small plastic containers. "These are perennials. They will come back every year if you care for them properly. These hostas are perennials that grow very well in the shade. These peonies are sun-loving perennials. Their flowers are nice."

"I'll start with some perennials, please. I don't see the point of growing something that may not return next year," said Pablo.

1 Unlike perennials, annuals
Ⓐ must be grown in hanging baskets.
Ⓑ cannot be grown in the sun.
Ⓒ need plenty of shade.
Ⓓ finish their life cycles in a year.

2 Which is an *opinion*?
Ⓐ Hostas grow well in the shade.
Ⓑ Hostas are a perennial.
Ⓒ Peonies grow well with lots of sun.
Ⓓ Peony flowers are nice.

E. When Jordy Brown was five, his dad came home from a trip to Mexico with a poster from a bullfight. Jordy thought it looked cruel. He made his dad promise never to go to a bullfight again. But Jordy didn't stop there. The eleven-year-old from Irvine, California, wanted to end bullfights for good. Jordy **launched** a letter-writing campaign and petition drive to convince Mexican leaders to stop bullfights. Jordy also adopted two baby bulls named Rocky and Ben. Jordy sends money to people who own the bulls to help care for them and keep them safe.

Jordy says anyone who looks into a bull's eyes knows it's a creature that deserves respect. "Bulls have beautiful eyes," Jordy says. "They are really sweet animals."

1 In this passage, the word **launched** means
Ⓐ sailed.   Ⓒ ended.
Ⓑ wrote.   Ⓓ began.

2 Jordy first learned about bullfights
Ⓐ on television.
Ⓑ when he saw two bulls up for adoption.
Ⓒ when his father came home from Mexico with a poster from a bullfight.
Ⓓ through a letter-writing campaign and petition drive.

Vocabulary

Synonyms

Read the underlined word in each phrase. Mark the word below it that has the same (or close to the same) meaning.

Sample:
essential equipment
- (A) necessary
- (B) expensive
- (C) cheap
- (D) sturdy

1 rigid material
- (A) stiff
- (B) red
- (C) natural
- (D) soft

2 elevate the book
- (A) read
- (B) criticize
- (C) describe
- (D) raise

3 became hysterical
- (A) emotional
- (B) calm
- (C) tired
- (D) energetic

4 a vague idea
- (A) bad
- (B) sketchy
- (C) new
- (D) great

5 an outlandish outfit
- (A) outgrown
- (B) handsome
- (C) silly
- (D) common

6 surprising triumph
- (A) solution
- (B) victory
- (C) friend
- (D) day

7 tattered clothing
- (A) colorful
- (B) new
- (C) worn-out
- (D) clean

Antonyms

Read the underlined word in each phrase. Mark the word below it that means the opposite or nearly the opposite.

Sample:
an efficient worker
- (A) busy
- (B) hard
- (C) wasteful
- (D) quick

1 a defiant attitude
- (A) unhappy
- (B) respectful
- (C) confused
- (D) poor

2 inferior brand
- (A) exterior
- (B) popular
- (C) superior
- (D) expensive

3 the courage to persist
- (A) speak
- (B) continue
- (C) act
- (D) quit

4 amateur athlete
- (A) gifted
- (B) competitive
- (C) professional
- (D) untalented

5 decline the offer
- (A) ignore
- (B) accept
- (C) debate
- (D) consider

6 valuable idea
- (A) useful
- (B) super
- (C) worthless
- (D) certain

7 nervous feeling
- (A) calm
- (B) frightened
- (C) angry
- (D) funny

Reading Skills Practice Test 2
Reading Comprehension

Read each passage. Then, fill in the circle that best completes each sentence or answers each question.

Is red just red and green just green? Apparently not, say **authorities** on color. In every culture, colors have meanings. And each culture looks at specific colors in different ways.

White, for example, is a popular choice for American wedding gowns. In China, however, brides prefer to wear red, which traditionally means joy and celebration in Chinese culture. For them, white is associated with mourning and wearing it at a wedding is considered unlucky.

Blue is the most accepted color around the world, authorities say. Few cultures assign blue a negative meaning, perhaps because it is the color of water and sky.

1 In this passage, the word **authorities** means
Ⓐ witnesses.
Ⓑ experts.
Ⓒ countries.
Ⓓ animals.

2 What is the best title for this passage?
Ⓐ "Water and Sky"
Ⓑ "Japanese Bridal Traditions"
Ⓒ "The Meaning of Blue"
Ⓓ "The Meaning of Colors"

A. Is there really a monster living deep in the beautiful Scottish lake? Those who claim that the Loch Ness monster exists point to strange disturbances in the water. Sometimes the surface ripples. It bubbles and shakes. Occasionally, a hump, like a dinosaur's, seems to appear.

An Italian scientist came up with a "non-monsterly" cause for these events. Luigi Piccardi points to the Great Glen Fault that runs under the lake. A fault is a fissure in Earth. Faults can cause gas eruptions, roaring sounds, and earthquakes. Piccardi believes that these kinds of things cause the disturbances, not a monster.

1 Luigi Piccardi maintains that
Ⓐ the Great Glen Fault explains Loch Ness monster sightings.
Ⓑ there are no disturbances in Loch Ness.
Ⓒ the Loch Ness monster exists.
Ⓓ the Loch Ness monster caused the Great Glen Fault.

2 Which of these is an *opinion*?
Ⓐ Faults can cause gas eruptions.
Ⓑ Disturbances have occurred in the surface of the lake.
Ⓒ The Great Glen Fault runs beneath Loch Ness.
Ⓓ The Loch Ness monster exists.

B. Experiencing nature is great, but when backpacking, fishing, or hiking in the woods always keep safety in mind. Remembering several important rules can keep a wilderness **excursion** from turning into tragedy.

First, be prepared for weather changes. Always pack warm clothes and rain wear, just in case! This is particularly true in the mountains. The weather at high altitude is notoriously fickle.

Second, carry a map, compass, and flashlight. Even experienced hikers get lost. You should be familiar with your route before you start your trip. Study the map to get to know the area and any landmarks along the way. The flashlight is important if you do get lost. Many trips that start out in daylight become nighttime adventures when people can't find their way.

Third, bring a first-aid kit and know how to use it. Small scrapes can be more serious when there is no doctor nearby. Finally, tell people where you are going and when you plan to come back. That way, someone will go look for you in case trouble strikes.

1 In this passage, the word **excursion** means
Ⓐ truck. Ⓒ outing.
Ⓑ vehicle. Ⓓ discussion.

2 The purpose of this passage is to
Ⓐ amuse. Ⓒ inform.
Ⓑ frighten. Ⓓ sell a product.

C. Talking on a hand-held phone while driving is a safety issue. When people pay attention to the phone, they don't pay attention to the road. This can lead to accidents and even deaths. According to one study, people who gab on the phone while driving may be four times more likely to get into an accident.

Today, no state has a complete ban on cell phone use for all drivers, but most states have some limitation on cell phone use. In 24 states, Washington, D.C., Puerto Rico, Guam, and the U.S. Virgin Islands, all drivers are prohibited from using hand-held cell phones while driving. Other states only ban cell phone use for new or teen drivers. However, most states agree on one thing—you should not text and drive. In 48 states, Washington, D.C., Puerto Rico, Guam and the U.S. Virgin Islands there is a ban on text messaging while driving for all drivers.

1 What is illegal in 48 states?
Ⓐ cell phone use while driving
Ⓑ text messaging while driving
Ⓒ cell phone use by experienced drivers
Ⓓ cell phone use by novice drivers

2 You can infer from this story that
Ⓐ all drivers now use cell phones.
Ⓑ soon all drivers will use cell phones.
Ⓒ driving in a car may become more dangerous.
Ⓓ more states may enact laws about cell phone use while driving.

D. "I could never possibly do it," I said. I meant it, seriously! My sister Pilar had been describing how much she loved scuba diving. We were spending two weeks at the beach, and she had just finished her initial underwater dive. She raved about the brightly colored coral, the anemones, the turtles, and even the shark that she had observed.

"It's like another world down there, James," said Pilar. "There's the world on dry land and the world beneath the water; the only way you can see that world is by putting on a scuba mask and oxygen tank. It's not actually dangerous. You get trained on the proper usage of the equipment, and the instructor is always present. If an emergency occurs, you're completely prepared."

"I don't care about another world," I replied, "I don't want to be eaten by sharks and what if I run out of oxygen? I'm a dry-land type of guy."

My sister is very **persistent**, however, and before the first week was up, I was enrolled in scuba instruction against my will. Pilar was waiting when I surfaced from my first dive. "Well?" she said. "Wow, Pilar. It is another world!" I shouted.

1 At first, how does James seem to feel about diving?
- Ⓐ excited
- Ⓑ terrified
- Ⓒ bored
- Ⓓ interested

2 In this passage, **persistent** means
- Ⓐ determined.
- Ⓑ prudent.
- Ⓒ agitated.
- Ⓓ calm.

E. Some people call it the Roof of the World. The country is Bhutan. It's a tiny kingdom high in the mountains of the Himalayas. Bhutan shares its borders with China and India, the world's two most populous countries. But compared with those giants, Bhutan is tiny. It's only about half the size of Indiana, and has fewer than one million inhabitants.

Bhutan means Land of the Thunder Dragon, a reference to the severe storms that roar through the Himalayas. These rugged mountains dominate the country. They also keep it isolated from the rest of the world. There are only two airlines that fly to Bhutan. Up until 1962, the country had no postal service or paved roads. The internet and television arrived in 1999.

Not many people get the chance to visit this tiny country, but those who do get to see the Bhutanese way of life, the mountains, and the forests. Bhutan has a remarkable diversity of wildlife, hundreds of species of birds, and 5,000 different types of plants.

1 Compared to India and China, Bhutan
- Ⓐ has a greater diversity of wildlife.
- Ⓑ has many visitors.
- Ⓒ is very modern.
- Ⓓ is a very small country.

2 Which happened most recently?
- Ⓐ Television arrived in Bhutan.
- Ⓑ Bhutan's first paved road was built.
- Ⓒ Bhutan became independent.
- Ⓓ Bhutan developed a postal service.

Vocabulary

Synonyms

Read the underlined word in each phrase.
Mark the word below it that has the same
(or close to the same) meaning.

Sample:
   <u>fabulous</u> recipe
   - Ⓐ excellent
   - Ⓒ difficult
   - Ⓑ tasteless
   - Ⓓ frivolous

1 <u>humiliating</u> event
   - Ⓐ successful
   - Ⓒ disturbing
   - Ⓑ embarrassing
   - Ⓓ frightening

2 <u>capable</u> hands
   - Ⓐ able
   - Ⓒ clumsy
   - Ⓑ unable
   - Ⓓ fast

3 looking for <u>insight</u>
   - Ⓐ contentment
   - Ⓒ courtesy
   - Ⓑ understanding
   - Ⓓ forgiveness

4 <u>supreme</u> confidence
   - Ⓐ absolute
   - Ⓒ surprising
   - Ⓑ little
   - Ⓓ inadequate

5 <u>acquire</u> knowledge
   - Ⓐ lose
   - Ⓒ reject
   - Ⓑ gain
   - Ⓓ reflect

6 take a <u>stroll</u>
   - Ⓐ look
   - Ⓒ board
   - Ⓑ number
   - Ⓓ walk

7 <u>waterfront</u> location
   - Ⓐ central
   - Ⓒ island
   - Ⓑ mountainous
   - Ⓓ shore

Antonyms

Read the underlined word in each phrase.
Mark the word below it that means the
opposite or nearly the opposite.

Sample:
   <u>artificial</u> flavoring
   - Ⓐ superficial
   - Ⓒ unusual
   - Ⓑ delicious
   - Ⓓ natural

1 <u>overtake</u> the leader
   - Ⓐ overwhelm
   - Ⓒ fall behind
   - Ⓑ obstruct
   - Ⓓ rejoin

2 <u>considerable</u> amount
   - Ⓐ strange
   - Ⓒ small
   - Ⓑ expensive
   - Ⓓ large

3 beg to <u>differ</u>
   - Ⓐ digest
   - Ⓒ agree
   - Ⓑ defer
   - Ⓓ assume

4 <u>betray</u> the cause
   - Ⓐ disturb
   - Ⓒ support
   - Ⓑ believe
   - Ⓓ understand

5 <u>reckless</u> behavior
   - Ⓐ careless
   - Ⓒ proud
   - Ⓑ careful
   - Ⓓ humble

6 <u>tighten</u> the hold
   - Ⓐ return
   - Ⓒ slow
   - Ⓑ remove
   - Ⓓ loosen

7 possible <u>solution</u>
   - Ⓐ problem
   - Ⓒ activity
   - Ⓑ surprise
   - Ⓓ idea

Name _____ Date _____

Reading Skills Practice Test 3
Reading Comprehension

Read each passage. Then, fill in the circle that best completes each sentence or answers each question.

SAMPLE

Fifty years ago, thousands of wild Siberian tigers roamed freely across a large part of Asia—in Siberia, China, and North and South Korea. Today, only about 400 of these great cats survive. Unless **drastic** measures are taken, the tiger may be extinct in the near future.

1 In this passage, the word **drastic** means
Ⓐ serious.　　Ⓒ small.
Ⓑ natural.　　Ⓓ many.

2 What is the best title for this passage?
Ⓐ "The Countries of Asia"
Ⓑ "Endangered Animals"
Ⓒ "Tigers Born in Zoos"
Ⓓ "The Siberian Tiger"

A.　California condors are the largest birds in North America. But these flying giants are in danger of dying out. Experts are trying to save condors by catching them and raising their young in a safe environment. When they are old enough, the condor chicks are released.

Scientists fear these condor chicks may not know enough about the dangers of life on their own. Some have flown into power lines—the wires and cables that carry electricity. Many young condors have gotten hurt or killed. Now, people in places where condors live want to bury power lines to keep condors safe.

1 What happens to some condors after they are released?
Ⓐ They fly to California.
Ⓑ They are raised by experts.
Ⓒ They hurt other animals.
Ⓓ They are hurt or killed.

2 You can guess that
Ⓐ people care about condors.
Ⓑ condors will soon die out.
Ⓒ power lines are too long.
Ⓓ there are too many condors.

3 Which of these is an *opinion* about condors?
Ⓐ They are birds.
Ⓑ They are in danger.
Ⓒ They live in the U.S.
Ⓓ They are ugly.

B. Hiking is a great way to exercise. On a hike you can enjoy beautiful scenery, observe interesting plants and animals, and build your muscles—especially if you walk uphill. But hiking can be dangerous, if you're not careful.

First, you should plan your hiking trip. Carry a good map and make sure you have comfortable shoes with thick soles. It's smart to carry water, and food too, if it's going to be a long hike. Finally, set a comfortable walking pace. Going too fast will tire you out quickly.

Being prepared makes hiking less dangerous and more fun. So lace up those hiking boots and pack up your knapsack. There's a lot of beautiful countryside out there.

1 What is the best title for this passage?
Ⓐ "How to Hike Safely"
Ⓑ "Good Hiking Shoes"
Ⓒ "Hiking Trails in Your Area"
Ⓓ "Where to Buy a Hiking Map"

2 Which of these is an *opinion*?
Ⓐ Hiking can build muscles.
Ⓑ Walking too fast can tire you out.
Ⓒ Hiking is the best way to exercise.
Ⓓ Tight shoes can cause blisters.

3 When hiking, which would you do last?
Ⓐ wear comfortable shoes
Ⓑ pack food and water
Ⓒ carry a map
Ⓓ walk at a comfortable pace

C. During the 1960s, women inspired by the civil rights movement realized they did not have the same rights and opportunities as men. So they started the women's movement. Soon two laws were passed. The Equal Pay Act was passed in 1963. It required that men and women in the same workplace be given equal pay for equal work. The Civil Rights Act of 1964 was a big victory for the civil rights movement and for women. That law made it illegal to discriminate against anyone because of skin color, religion, or gender.

Today, women make up more than half the U.S. workforce. They have moved into jobs that were not open to women in the past. Women work as astronauts, construction workers, executives, engineers, and firefighters. However, there is still more work to do—many women are still paid less than men for equal work.

1 Why was the women's movement started?
Ⓐ Some women didn't have families.
Ⓑ Women had too many rights.
Ⓒ Women wanted to work.
Ⓓ Women wanted the same rights and opportunities as men.

2 Which happened last?
Ⓐ The Civil Rights Act was passed.
Ⓑ Women realized that they did not have the same rights as men.
Ⓒ The civil rights movement started.
Ⓓ Women became more than half the workforce.

D.   Since ancient times, people all over the world have loved mountains. That's because mountains are some of the most beautiful landforms. They exist, in different shapes and sizes, on every continent.

Probably, the four best-known mountain ranges are the Himalayas in Asia, the Andes in South America, the Alps in Europe, and the Rockies in North America. All of these great ranges are different.

The Himalayas contain many of the world's tallest mountains, including Mount Everest—the tallest mountain in the world at 29,032 feet. In contrast, Mont Blanc, the tallest of the Alps, is only 15,771 feet. The Rockies are home to native North American wildlife such as bison and bighorn sheep, while the Andes are home to llama, alpaca and other camelids.

1 According to the passage, how are the Alps different from the Himalayas?
Ⓐ The Alps are taller.
Ⓑ The Alps are more arid.
Ⓒ The Alps are smaller.
Ⓓ The Alps contain more wildlife.

2 The main idea of this passage is
Ⓐ only the Rockies contain wildlife.
Ⓑ people like the Alps much more than the Himalayas.
Ⓒ the Andes are less beautiful than the Rockies.
Ⓓ mountain ranges are beautiful and unique landforms.

E.   Once upon a time in India, a wise man named Sessa invented the game of chess. The maharaja, or king, liked this new game very much and said to Sessa, "Ask for anything in my kingdom and it shall be yours."

Sessa bowed his head. "Your Majesty," he said, "all I ask for is as many grains of rice as would fill the 64 squares of a chessboard, if one grain were put in the first square, two grains in the second, four in the third, eight in the fourth, and so on, doubling the number for each new square."

The king said, "Sessa, you deserve much more, but I will grant your **humble** request." A few days later, one of the maharaja's advisors said, "Your majesty, we cannot give Sessa his reward. The total amount of rice came to 18,446,744,073,709,551,615 grains! That's more rice than we have in the entire kingdom."

1 The purpose of this passage is to
Ⓐ entertain.   Ⓒ persuade.
Ⓑ advertise.   Ⓓ protest.

2 In this passage, **humble** means
Ⓐ modest.   Ⓒ grand.
Ⓑ shallow.   Ⓓ bold.

3 According to the passage, how many grains of rice go in the fourth square of the chessboard?
Ⓐ two   Ⓒ eight
Ⓑ four   Ⓓ twelve

Vocabulary
Which Word Is Missing?
In each of the following paragraphs, a word is missing. First, read each paragraph. Then choose the missing word from the list beneath the paragraph. Fill in the circle next to the word that is missing.

Sample:

Curtis likes his room to be _____. He puts his clothes away, makes his bed, and keeps papers piled neatly on his desk.

  Ⓐ messy   Ⓒ smart

  Ⓑ tidy   Ⓓ shy

❶ The problem of endangered _____ is very serious. Unless we act now, many plants and animals could become extinct.

  Ⓐ areas   Ⓒ pets

  Ⓑ species   Ⓓ spires

❷ Although the problem is _____, we shouldn't let its size keep us from taking action.

  Ⓐ miniature   Ⓒ formidable

  Ⓑ resolute   Ⓓ reliable

❸ According to _____, there are several reasons that animals and plants become endangered. These experts should know. They study the delicate balance between life and the environment.

  Ⓐ ecologists   Ⓒ zookeepers

  Ⓑ engineers   Ⓓ gardeners

❹ Animals become endangered when their _____ is drastically changed or destroyed. Humans are often the cause.

  Ⓐ echo   Ⓒ family

  Ⓑ habitat   Ⓓ hazard

❺ If people around the world _____, we can help protect these plants and animals. But we must work together.

  Ⓐ muster   Ⓒ manipulate

  Ⓑ pledge   Ⓓ cooperate

❻ Did you know that _____ plays a large part in many highway accidents? That's because people often keep driving even though they are tired. This can be as dangerous as driving drunk.

  Ⓐ finance   Ⓒ destiny

  Ⓑ fatigue   Ⓓ depression

❼ When doing _____ driving, people should plan to stop, stretch, and rest every few hours. It's worth the extra time it takes to make these stops because they can help keep drivers alert.

  Ⓐ long-dead   Ⓒ long-distance

  Ⓑ long-handled   Ⓓ long-legged

Reading Skills Practice Test 4
Reading Comprehension

Read each passage. Then, fill in the circle that best completes each sentence or answers each question.

SAMPLE

What do you get when you cross a camel with a llama? The answer is not the punchline of a new joke. It's actually a new animal called a cama. Llamas produce nice wool, but camels are bigger. So, scientists hope the cama will be a big wool producer!

1 A cama is
- Ⓐ a small camel.
- Ⓑ a cross between a camel and a llama.
- Ⓒ a very special type of llama.
- Ⓓ a new animal that lays eggs.

2 What is one difference between camels and llamas?
- Ⓐ Camels are meaner.
- Ⓑ Llamas are taller.
- Ⓒ Camels are bigger.
- Ⓓ Llamas don't produce wool.

A. How would you feel if you never saw a saguaro cactus again? You might not care, but the lesser long-nosed bats that depend on saguaro cactus blossoms for food sure would. They thrive on the cantaloupe-scented, cream-white blossoms that open each night to the desert air.

The Gila Woodpecker and the Gilded Flicker would care a lot as well. Both of these birds drill small holes in cactus trunks for their homes.

Without bats to pollinate them, the cactus can't reproduce. Ten types of bats that feed on cactus blossoms are already extinct. The lesser long-nosed bat is on the endangered list. Scientists are afraid the saguaro cactus is not far behind.

1 What would prevent the cactus from reproducing?
- Ⓐ the extinction of bats that pollinate them
- Ⓑ birds drilling too many holes for homes in the cactus
- Ⓒ long-nosed bats eating all the cactus blossoms
- Ⓓ cactus blossoms not producing enough pollen to reproduce

2 The next paragraph is likely to be about
- Ⓐ other endangered species.
- Ⓑ how people are trying to save the cactus.
- Ⓒ different birds of the desert.
- Ⓓ the many different scents of cactus blossoms.

B. In 2028, when the new millennium is over a quarter-century old, an asteroid is expected to whiz past Earth. But despite early reports, there's no need to worry. The closest it will come is 600,000 miles—more than twice as far away as the moon.

Asteroids are large rocks that revolve around the sun between the orbits of Mars and Jupiter. Some are as small as a TV set. Others are as wide as the length of California. At one mile wide, the asteroid passing by Earth in 2028 is medium-size.

First reports said the asteroid could come close enough to possibly hit Earth—an event that could cause deadly tidal waves and climate problems. Fortunately, new information has shown that Earth is definitely not in danger.

1 What is the best title for this passage?
Ⓐ "Asteroid Approaches Earth"
Ⓑ "The End of Earth"
Ⓒ "How Asteroids Are Formed"
Ⓓ "Life in 2028"

2 How close will the asteroid pass to Earth?
Ⓐ closer than the moon
Ⓑ 400,000 miles
Ⓒ as close as Mars
Ⓓ 600,000 miles

3 According to the passage, which of the following might happen if the asteroid hit Earth?
Ⓐ a world war   Ⓒ tidal waves
Ⓑ forest fires   Ⓓ famine

C. At 7:00 a.m. (Nepalese time) on May 27, 1998, Tom Whittaker fulfilled the dream of his life. After a grueling eight-hour trek up **treacherous** rock and ice, Whittaker made it to the top of the world. He had climbed Mount Everest!

Whittaker was no ordinary climber. He lost his right foot and kneecap in a car accident in 1979. When he reached Mount Everest's summit, he became the first disabled person ever to successfully scale the world's tallest peak. Not bad for someone who days before was told by doctors he'd die if he didn't give up his climb—and his dream.

But, after considering the doctors' advice carefully, Whittaker and his team decided to keep going for their dream. So on a May morning, Whittaker stood at 29,028 feet (8848 meters)—literally on top of the world. What was he thinking? "Thank God there's no more up in front of me!"

1 What did Tom Whittaker do?
Ⓐ He became the first disabled person to climb Mount Everest.
Ⓑ He survived the world's worst car accident.
Ⓒ He climbed Mount Everest without permission.
Ⓓ He climbed Mount Everest without a team or other supporters.

2 In this passage the word **treacherous** means
Ⓐ dangerous.   Ⓒ freezing.
Ⓑ mean.   Ⓓ wonderful.

D. There are two types of garbage. Natural garbage such as an apple core is biodegradable. It will rot over time. Manufactured garbage, such as a plastic bag, is not biodegradable. It will stay the same for hundreds of years. Luckily, much of our manufactured garbage can be recycled. This will **prevent** our planet from filling up with trash. To find out if your trash is biodegradable, try this test:

1. Fill several flowerpots with damp soil.
2. Find some small pieces of garbage.
3. Bury one piece of garbage in each flowerpot.
4. Write labels to show what is buried in each flowerpot.
5. Place the pots in a cool, damp place.
6. After a few weeks, dig up the buried pieces of garbage. Which pieces didn't rot? Check to see if your community recycles this type of trash.

1 In this passage, the word **prevent** means
Ⓐ stop. Ⓒ help.
Ⓑ grow. Ⓓ build.

2 What should you do right after you put the pots in a cool place?
Ⓐ bury pieces of trash
Ⓑ wait a few weeks
Ⓒ find some flowerpots
Ⓓ dig up the garbage

3 You would probably find this passage in a book about
Ⓐ flowerpots. Ⓒ dirt.
Ⓑ recycling. Ⓓ aluminum.

E. This excerpt is from an essay by Lauren Gleason, 13.

"Sometimes, the strangest things can be your friend." So my Grandma once said. Until now, I never understood what she meant. I have a best friend, but it is not another girl to giggle with. My friend cannot make me up to look like a movie star, curl luscious **locks** into my hair, or be the holder of my deepest, darkest secrets. Nor is my friend a dog, a loyal companion that follows its master far and wide and depends on him as a kitten does its mother for milk.

The thing where I go to seek friendship (for it never tells a lie and is always there) is a rickety, old porch swing that hangs from my porch roof by rusted chains hooked to oversize screws. Its wooden seat is just long enough for me to stretch my whole body out upon. The grains in the wood ripple in all directions, creating odd, circle-shaped figures. I always pay a visit to the swing when I'm lonely, angry, worried, or upset."

1 In this passage, **locks** means
Ⓐ strands. Ⓒ colors.
Ⓑ bows. Ⓓ flowers.

2 The best description of the porch swing is
Ⓐ sparkling and new.
Ⓑ old and decrepit.
Ⓒ clean and shiny.
Ⓓ safe and well-maintained.

Vocabulary

Synonyms

Read the underlined word in each phrase. Mark the word below it that has the same (or close to the same) meaning.

Sample:
grave consequence
- (A) action
- (C) consent
- (B) result
- (D) solution

1 customary procedure
- (A) normal
- (C) precise
- (B) strange
- (D) follow

2 formidable foe
- (A) friend
- (C) task
- (B) obstacle
- (D) enemy

3 illuminate the building
- (A) shut down
- (C) light up
- (B) fix up
- (D) turn off

4 sharp talons
- (A) tongues
- (C) claws
- (B) edges
- (D) teeth

5 gape at
- (A) sneer
- (C) smile
- (B) squint
- (D) stare

6 toxic substance
- (A) nutritious
- (C) poisonous
- (B) added
- (D) bitter

7 considerate behavior
- (A) rude
- (C) aggressive
- (B) thoughtful
- (D) meek

Antonyms

Read the underlined word in each phrase. Mark the word below it that means the opposite or nearly the opposite.

Sample:
dejected expression
- (A) sad
- (C) angry
- (B) happy
- (D) sorrowful

1 evident difference
- (A) obvious
- (C) unmentionable
- (B) unnoticeable
- (D) unlikely

2 glum look
- (A) sad
- (C) troubled
- (B) gleeful
- (D) unhappy

3 meek person
- (A) aggressive
- (C) creative
- (B) polite
- (D) dangerous

4 overcast day
- (A) rainy
- (C) sunny
- (B) dark
- (D) snowy

5 torment him
- (A) torture
- (C) obey
- (B) soothe
- (D) insult

6 impulsive action
- (A) spontaneous
- (C) unwise
- (B) considered
- (D) intelligent

7 festive occasion
- (A) official
- (C) cheerful
- (B) unplanned
- (D) somber

Reading Skills Practice Test 5
Reading Comprehension

Read each passage. Then, fill in the circle that best completes each sentence or answers each question.

SAMPLE

The World Series is baseball's biggest event. Each year, fans **applaud** the winners. When the Boston Red Sox won in 2002, fans applauded even more than usual. Pitcher Jon Lester's performance was nothing short of amazing. Earlier that year, doctors treated Lester for cancer. Not only did he beat cancer, but he battled back to become the World Series' winning pitcher.

1 In this passage the word **applaud** means
  Ⓐ cheer for.
  Ⓑ remember.
  Ⓒ award.
  Ⓓ fulfill.

2 What is the best title for this passage?
  Ⓐ "Champions of the World Series"
  Ⓑ "Jon Lester's Incredible Victory"
  Ⓒ "Baseball Winners"
  Ⓓ "Jon Lester's Fastball"

A.   In some places, fishermen use cyanide to catch fish. Cyanide is a deadly poison. Fishermen dump cyanide into the ocean, stunning big fish. The fish float to the surface where they are easy to catch. Unfortunately, cyanide fishing is a disaster for the environment.

Cyanide doesn't just stun fish; it kills the coral reefs in which fish live. Reefs are one of the most beautiful of all ecosystems. They take centuries to grow, so the damage caused by cyanide lasts for years. Without the coral, many ocean fish lose food sources and nesting grounds. With less coral, there will be fewer fish. In effect, the fishermen are poisoning their own future.

1 Why do some fishermen use cyanide?
  Ⓐ They want to kill coral.
  Ⓑ Cyanide makes it easy to catch big fish.
  Ⓒ They are trying to rebuild damaged reefs.
  Ⓓ It's the only way they can catch fish.

2 Which of these is an *opinion*?
  Ⓐ Coral reefs take centuries to grow.
  Ⓑ Cyanide use will soon be stopped.
  Ⓒ Reefs are one of the most beautiful of all ecosystems.
  Ⓓ In some places, fishermen use cyanide to catch fish.

B. Albert Einstein was born in Germany in 1879. As a child, few people guessed that he was going to be a famous scientist whose theories would change the world. He was slow in school, and some teachers thought he wasn't very bright.

When he grew up, Einstein wanted to be a science teacher—but nobody would hire him. He didn't give up, however, and went on to develop ideas about time and energy that changed science. One theory explained the way light beams travel, which made TV possible!

Einstein won the Nobel prize in 1921. In 1933 he fled from Nazi Germany and came to America. Here, he worked on atomic energy with other scientists. Although the atom bomb helped the U.S. end World War II, Einstein was always against using atomic energy to harm people. After the war, he worked for international peace.

1 Which of these events occurred last?
Ⓐ Einstein won the Nobel prize.
Ⓑ Einstein worked on atomic energy with scientists in America.
Ⓒ Einstein fled Nazi Germany.
Ⓓ Einstein worked for international peace.

2 Einstein fled Germany because
Ⓐ he couldn't get a job.
Ⓑ he wanted to be a science teacher.
Ⓒ of the Nazis.
Ⓓ of the atomic bomb.

C. People who live in Death Valley definitely know the meaning of the word hot. In summer, they wear gloves to avoid frying their fingers on car door handles. To keep candles from melting, they store them in their refrigerators. Some folks here even give their babies ice cubes for toys. That's because they live in the hottest and lowest spot in the Western Hemisphere!

Death Valley lies 282 feet below sea level and can get as hot as 134 degrees Fahrenheit in the summer. It gets so hot that rain evaporates even before it touches the ground! Not that there is much rain to worry about in Death Valley. The bone-dry valley gets less than two inches of rainfall a year.

Despite its grim name, Death Valley contains 900 kinds of plants. There are also lots of animals. Bobcats, coyotes, and reptiles hide in the sand during the sweltering heat of the day and come out at night when it gets cooler.

1 Bobcats, coyotes, and reptiles hide in the sand
Ⓐ to avoid people.
Ⓑ to avoid cars.
Ⓒ because of the rain.
Ⓓ because of the heat.

2 The main idea of this passage is that
Ⓐ people shouldn't live in Death Valley.
Ⓑ there are 900 kinds of plants in Death Valley.
Ⓒ Death Valley is the lowest spot in the Western Hemisphere.
Ⓓ Death Valley is incredibly hot.

D. The next time you walk by the candy aisle in the grocery store, stop for a moment and think about how each candy got invented. Who decided to make that candy cherry-tangerine flavored, or this one wild-berry surprise?

Chances are, it was a candy chemist. Candy chemists invent new flavors of candy. And while it may be fun, it's not that easy. They have over 2,000 different ingredients to taste and work with. The pressure is on to come up with new and inventive flavors that are also delicious.

A surprising number of ingredients go into a flavor of candy. As they search for that perfect ingredient mix, candy chemists come face-to-face with the hardest part of their job. They have to taste everything, even the rejects!

1 What do candy chemists do?
Ⓐ They stock the candy aisles in supermarkets.
Ⓑ They invent new flavors of candy.
Ⓒ They eat a lot of candy and choose a favorite.
Ⓓ They search for the perfect candy.

2 Which of these is an *opinion*?
Ⓐ A candy chemist's job is not easy.
Ⓑ Candy chemists work with over 2,000 ingredients.
Ⓒ Candy chemists must come up with new and delicious flavors.
Ⓓ A lot of ingredients go into a flavor of candy.

E. When Prakesh first saw the bicycle in the store window, he couldn't believe it. It looked just like the one in the magazine he had seen back home in India. Somehow, seeing it made him realize he was **destined** to have this bike.

He began figuring out how long it would take him to buy it. The bike cost $499. He made $40 a week working part time for his uncle at the restaurant. He already had $120 in the bank. That meant he could buy the bike in 10 weeks. But what if someone else bought it first? Prakesh decided to see if the store would put it on layaway for him.

When he asked, the store clerk just smiled at him. "There's more than one of those bikes. I can order one for you at any time," he told Prakesh. "Why don't you let me know about two weeks before you have all the money. I'll order the bike for you then."

Prakesh couldn't wait. In just a few weeks he would be biking all over town!

1 In this passage, **destined** means
Ⓐ fated.   Ⓒ not allowed.
Ⓑ unable.   Ⓓ sorry.

2 You can infer from this passage that Prakesh
Ⓐ had wanted a bike for a very long time.
Ⓑ didn't work very hard at his job.
Ⓒ didn't know how to ride a bike.
Ⓓ didn't like working at his uncle's restaurant.

Vocabulary

Synonyms

Read the underlined word in each phrase. Mark the word below it that has the same (or close to the same) meaning.

Sample:

propose a plan
- (A) reveal
- (B) reject
- (C) deny
- (D) suggest

1. heavy luggage
- (A) weight
- (B) clothing
- (C) load
- (D) baggage

2. holiday fiesta
- (A) party
- (B) gift
- (C) time
- (D) spirit

3. speedy getaway
- (A) path
- (B) automobile
- (C) escape
- (D) gateway

4. humiliating experience
- (A) merciless
- (B) unique
- (C) unusual
- (D) embarrassing

5. endless quest
- (A) fountain
- (B) search
- (C) passage
- (D) prank

6. acute pain
- (A) dull
- (B) minor
- (C) sharp
- (D) sudden

7. predicted storm
- (A) understood
- (B) foreseen
- (C) unforeseen
- (D) intense

Antonyms

Read the underlined word in each phrase. Mark the word below it that means the opposite or nearly the opposite.

Sample:

unfortunate event
- (A) important
- (B) early
- (C) late
- (D) lucky

1. hostile crowd
- (A) savage
- (B) friendly
- (C) obedient
- (D) humble

2. foster learning
- (A) support
- (B) allow
- (C) encourage
- (D) discourage

3. radiant colors
- (A) glowing
- (B) light
- (C) dull
- (D) bright

4. clammy cave
- (A) hidden
- (B) underground
- (C) cold and windy
- (D) hot and dry

5. abstract concept
- (A) unoriginal
- (B) original
- (C) concrete
- (D) exceptional

6. precious metal
- (A) rare
- (B) valuable
- (C) soft
- (D) common

7. imprecise answer
- (A) exact
- (B) uncertain
- (C) thoughtless
- (D) vague

Reading Skills Practice Test 6
Reading Comprehension

Read each passage. Then, fill in the circle that best completes each sentence or answers each question.

SAMPLE

On the morning of November 14, 1963, the crew on a fishing boat off the coast of Iceland watched an unusual birth—the birth of an island! A dark smoky mass rose out of the water from a volcano that was erupting beneath the ocean. The new island was named Surtsey. Even today, it continues to grow from erupting lava.

1 What is the best title for this passage?
- Ⓐ "Volcanoes and Earthquakes"
- Ⓑ "An Island Is Born"
- Ⓒ "The People of Iceland"
- Ⓓ "Iceland's Fishing Industry"

2 From the passage, you can infer that
- Ⓐ lava forms some islands.
- Ⓑ Iceland is a volcanic island.
- Ⓒ volcanoes can form anywhere.
- Ⓓ the fishing boat's owner was named Surtsey.

A. Around 450 years ago, a baker in an Italian village put some tomatoes on flattened bread and called his creation pizza. Two hundred years later, someone added cheese. No one knows when pepperoni was first added. What we do know is that, today, Americans **consume** more than 30 million slices of pizza a day. And those are just the slices sold in restaurants!

Pizzas through the ages have had one thing in common: They are often baked directly on the hot floor of a stone oven. Why? The stone used in ovens is porous, or full of tiny holes. That means it can soak up water from the crust as the pizza bakes, so the pizza bottom gets crispy.

1 In this passage, the word **consume** means
- Ⓐ prepare.   Ⓒ make.
- Ⓑ sell.   Ⓓ eat.

2 You can infer from this passage that
- Ⓐ the inventor of pizza is famous.
- Ⓑ not all pizza is sold in restaurants.
- Ⓒ most people dislike crispy crusts.
- Ⓓ people didn't like cheese on pizza.

3 A pizza crust becomes crispy when
- Ⓐ cheese covers the crust.
- Ⓑ cheese absorbs water in the crust.
- Ⓒ the stone oven absorbs water from the crust.
- Ⓓ the stone oven releases water into the crust.

B. How far back can you trace your family tree? If you were Adrian Targett, you could go back 300 generations!

Scientists have discovered that Targett is a direct descendant of Cheddar Man. That's the name given to a 9,000-year-old skeleton found in a cave in the town of Cheddar, England. (Yes, they make cheese there.) "I've been in the cave a few times," says Targett, "but I never realized it was home to one of my ancestors."

How did Targett discover Cheddar Man was his ancestor? Scientists tested Cheddar Man's DNA and then compared it to the DNA of people from the town. When they compared Cheddar Man's DNA with Targett's, they discovered the two men were related.

1 How did scientists discover that Cheddar Man and Targett are related?
Ⓐ They had both men make cheese.
Ⓑ They compared the men's bones.
Ⓒ They compared the men's DNA.
Ⓓ They discovered that both men lived in caves.

2 What is the purpose of this passage?
Ⓐ to inform you about Cheddar Man's descendant
Ⓑ to persuade you that cheddar is a great cheese
Ⓒ to entertain you with facts about Cheddar Man
Ⓓ to convince you that DNA is not reliable

C. New Beginnings

we haven't spoken in over a year
it kind of scares me that it doesn't matter as much anymore
I went up the hill
there was this new girl from Boston
planting flowers where we used to sit
when I volunteered to help
she smiled and handed me some seeds
with a small shovel
she told me I could take some home with me and I smiled at her
as I started to walk back
I stuffed my pockets full of new beginnings
by Jennifer Chiou

1 What does the poem's narrator do after she smiles at the girl?
Ⓐ She goes up the hill.
Ⓑ She gets some seeds.
Ⓒ She volunteers to help.
Ⓓ She walks back.

2 In the poem, the seeds represent
Ⓐ flowers.   Ⓒ old friends.
Ⓑ new beginnings.   Ⓓ a garden.

3 You can guess from this poem that
Ⓐ the narrator and the girl are old friends.
Ⓑ the narrator doesn't like the new girl.
Ⓒ the narrator is dealing with the loss of a friendship.
Ⓓ there are no hills where the narrator lives.

D. One of the most spectacular sights in China isn't a city, a snow-capped peak, or a desert sand dune. It's a wall! To be more **precise**, it's the Great Wall, an ancient structure that took thousands of workers more than 40 years to build.

Most of the Great Wall was built between 259 and 210 B.C., during the reign of Emperor Qin Shihuang. He was a powerful leader who united many small states into a strong empire. He built the wall to protect his empire against Mongol horsemen who swept down from the north, raiding villages and towns. At an average of 25 feet tall and almost 13,000 miles long, the Great Wall of China is the longest structure ever built.

1 Ch'in Shih Huang Ti built the wall to
(A) keep people from escaping.
(B) employ thousands of workers.
(C) protect his empire.
(D) unite China.

2 In this passage, the word **precise** means
(A) exact.   (C) serious.
(B) bold.   (D) sensible.

3 You can infer from the passage that
(A) Ch'in Shih Huang Ti was nice.
(B) the Great Wall is an important historical structure.
(C) China has no sand dunes.
(D) Mongols lived south of Ch'in Shih Huang Ti's empire.

E. Imagine being able to switch on lights or television sets just by using your brain. It's not science fiction. Scientists in Australia are now testing an invention that could allow people to do just that!

How does it work? The human brain runs on tiny bits of electricity. When people are relaxed, most of the brain's electricity is a type called alpha waves. To capture brain power, scientists attach wires to people's heads and tell the people to relax. The wires pick up alpha waves and run them through a machine that makes the waves thousands of times stronger. Then the waves flick a switch that can control a light, a TV, an electric toy car, or other gadget. Experts hope this discovery will help disabled people who can't control switches with their hands.

1 The main idea of this passage is that
(A) people are usually relaxed.
(B) when people are relaxed, their brains produce alpha waves.
(C) an invention may let the brain switch appliances on and off.
(D) electricity travels in waves.

2 You can guess from this passage that
(A) scientists are still perfecting this invention.
(B) all animals make alpha waves.
(C) most people cannot relax.
(D) people watch a lot of TV.

Vocabulary

Synonyms

Read the underlined word in each phrase. Mark the word below it that has the same (or close to the same) meaning.

Sample:

amble along
- (A) run
- (B) stroll
- (C) jog
- (D) skip

1 gnaw a bone
- (A) chew
- (B) swallow
- (C) spit out
- (D) lick

2 erect posture
- (A) slumped
- (B) upright
- (C) bent
- (D) slouching

3 former president
- (A) current
- (B) previous
- (C) next
- (D) future

4 vacant house
- (A) occupied
- (B) empty
- (C) old
- (D) big

5 reveal the truth
- (A) show
- (B) hide
- (C) fight
- (D) embrace

6 drastic measure
- (A) extreme
- (B) ineffective
- (C) effective
- (D) costly

7 sensitive child
- (A) timid
- (B) easily hurt
- (C) tough
- (D) quiet

Antonyms

Read the underlined word in each phrase. Mark the word below it that means the opposite or nearly the opposite.

Sample:

elegant clothes
- (A) casual
- (B) formal
- (C) new
- (D) old

1 pester someone
- (A) meet
- (B) contact
- (C) bother
- (D) delight

2 lousy idea
- (A) great
- (B) terrible
- (C) creative
- (D) silly

3 vivid colors
- (A) dull
- (B) bright
- (C) pastel
- (D) loud

4 suitable outfit
- (A) inappropriate
- (B) perfect
- (C) ugly
- (D) coordinated

5 deny all charges
- (A) admit
- (B) laugh
- (C) write
- (D) spend

6 flammable cloth
- (A) aflame
- (B) flimsy
- (C) fireproof
- (D) stiff

7 homely appearance
- (A) plain
- (B) attractive
- (C) ugly
- (D) unattractive

Reading Skills Practice Test 7
Reading Comprehension

Read each passage. Then, fill in the circle that best completes each sentence or answers each question.

In his 20s, Tiger Woods was already being called one of the greatest athletes of our time. This **exceptional** golfer has broken numerous records. He's so famous that people use only his first name when they talk about him.

1 In this passage the word **exceptional** means
Ⓐ accepting.
Ⓑ really talented.
Ⓒ precise.
Ⓓ young.

2 What is the best title for this passage?
Ⓐ "Golf in America"
Ⓑ "Exceptional Athletes"
Ⓒ "The World's Most Famous Tiger"
Ⓓ "People Without Last Names"

A. The Vikings struck fear in the hearts of all who heard of them. These fearsome warriors and masters of the sea stole, slashed, and burned their way through life. However, most of Europe hadn't heard of the Vikings before 793 A.D. That's when Viking warriors sailed to England and launched an attack on wealthy English monks. This was the beginning of 300 years of Viking domination of Northern Europe.

But the Vikings had a less bloodthirsty side, as well. They were amazing sailors and explorers, and one of them, Leif Eriksson, led a ship whose crew became the first Europeans to land in North America. They also settled the cold islands of Greenland and Iceland in the North Atlantic.

1 Most of Europe learned about the Vikings
Ⓐ 300 years ago.
Ⓑ 700 years ago.
Ⓒ when Vikings settled Greenland.
Ⓓ in 793 A.D.

2 The passage will likely go on to discuss
Ⓐ wildlife in Greenland and Iceland.
Ⓑ English monks.
Ⓒ Leif Eriksson's life.
Ⓓ the settlement of North America.

3 You can guess that the Vikings
Ⓐ were short.
Ⓑ were sometimes violent.
Ⓒ took over Europe.
Ⓓ were not very smart.

B. Did you ever eat something that didn't agree with you? If you were a frog, it would not have been a problem. When frogs accidentally eat a poisonous insect, they get rid of it the hard way—they throw up their whole stomachs!

"Frogs aren't picky about what they swallow," explains biologist Richard Wassersug. "They take in a lot of food at one time, and sometimes they eat something **toxic**."

When this happens, a frog turns its stomach inside out and expels it through its esophagus (the tube that connects the mouth and stomach). The frog then wipes off the poison and swallows its stomach back down.

1 What is the best title for this passage?
Ⓐ "How Frogs Deal With Upset Stomachs"
Ⓑ "Common Frog Poisons"
Ⓒ "Animal Stomachs"
Ⓓ "Frogs Have No Necks"

2 In this passage, the word **toxic** means
Ⓐ delicious.　　Ⓒ large.
Ⓑ awful.　　Ⓓ poisonous.

3 What happens after a frog throws up its stomach?
Ⓐ It goes to sleep.
Ⓑ It grows another stomach.
Ⓒ It wipes off the poison.
Ⓓ It dies.

C. Early in the 1800s, Japan wanted nothing to do with the outside world. Its policy of isolation dated to 1639. Before that, Japan had traded with European countries. But Japan's rulers feared that those countries might try to take over Japan, so they stopped the trading.

For two centuries, Japan was mostly cut off from the outside world. Its rulers allowed only limited trade with nearby Asian countries and with the Dutch.

During that time, foreign ships could not stop at Japanese ports—not even for food or fuel. Then, in 1853, U.S. Navy Commodore Matthew Perry negotiated with the Japanese and helped to open up the country. Today, Japan is one of the world's most technologically advanced societies, and its economy depends upon trade with other countries.

1 This passage is mostly about
Ⓐ the history of trading in Japan.
Ⓑ modern technology in Japan.
Ⓒ different kinds of Japanese ships.
Ⓓ economies of Asian countries.

2 Why was Japan closed to the outside world?
Ⓐ They didn't have goods to trade.
Ⓑ Japan was too far away.
Ⓒ Japan's rulers were afraid Japan would be taken over.
Ⓓ Japan's rulers didn't like the Dutch.

3 The purpose of this passage is to
Ⓐ inform.　　Ⓒ persuade.
Ⓑ entertain.　　Ⓓ convince.

D.   Eighteen-year-old Billy Campbell was riding fast and hard. His horse was exhausted. Campbell hated to push the poor creature, but he was determined to make it to the next station faster than ever before.

He made it! Usually, Campbell liked to take a minute to relax at the station, but not this time. He grabbed his saddlebags and leaped off his horse. Seconds later, he and his precious cargo—news from the nation's capital—were on a new horse, continuing their journey west.

Campbell took part in a record-breaking feat in March 1861. That is when Pony Express riders carried the words of a speech by President Abraham Lincoln from St. Joseph, Missouri, to Sacramento, California, in 7 days and 17 hours. It was one of the most exciting rides ever!

1 What was Campbell carrying?
Ⓐ a sidesaddle
Ⓑ medical supplies
Ⓒ food
Ⓓ a speech

2 Which of these is an *opinion*?
Ⓐ Campbell had a very exciting ride.
Ⓑ Campbell carried saddlebags.
Ⓒ Campbell's horse was exhausted.
Ⓓ Campbell was traveling west.

3 From this passage you can guess that
Ⓐ mail should be delivered by horse.
Ⓑ Billy Campbell was not a good rider.
Ⓒ Lincoln's speech was very important.
Ⓓ Lincoln's speech was not important.

E.   Other than natural-history museums, Antarctica is the best place to hunt for meteorites, or space rocks, that crash into Earth. The Antarctic Search for Meteorites program (ANSMET) has been working since 1976 to recover meteorites that have fallen to Earth. On average they recover about 550 meteorites a year.

Why are so many meteorites found in Antarctica? Geologist Ralph Harvey says it's because Antarctica is a **vast** stretch of white ice and snow. Meteorites easily show up on such a surface.

Meteorites in Antarctica are first covered by layers of snow. Packed in under pressure, the snow turns to ice. Over thousands of years, the ice spreads out toward the edges of the continent and usually breaks off as icebergs. As the ice disappears, meteorites show up on the surface, just waiting to be found by the ANSMET team.

1 According to the passage, what happens first?
Ⓐ icebergs break off
Ⓑ snow turns to ice
Ⓒ meteorites show up on the surface
Ⓓ meteorites are covered by snow

2 In this passage, **vast** means
Ⓐ icy.   Ⓒ cold.
Ⓑ rocky.   Ⓓ large.

3 About how many meteorites does ANSMET find a year?
Ⓐ thousands   Ⓒ about 550
Ⓑ a few   Ⓓ less than 350

Vocabulary

Synonyms

Read the underlined word in each phrase. Mark the word below it that has the same (or close to the same) meaning.

Sample:
   <u>fatal</u> accident
   - A bad
   - B minor
   - C deadly
   - D traffic

1 <u>clash</u> of ideas
   - A collision
   - B failure
   - C ruin
   - D downpour

2 <u>tidy</u> room
   - A neat
   - B messy
   - C large
   - D cluttered

3 <u>gleeful</u> cry
   - A miserable
   - B frightened
   - C scary
   - D happy

4 <u>serene</u> expression
   - A unhappy
   - B peaceful
   - C serious
   - D stern

5 <u>muster</u> the energy
   - A expend
   - B store up
   - C gather up
   - D release

6 <u>abbreviate</u> the word
   - A say
   - B shorten
   - C write
   - D lose

7 <u>distribute</u> papers
   - A read
   - B organize
   - C sell
   - D give out

Antonyms

Read the underlined word in each phrase. Mark the word below it that means the opposite or nearly the opposite.

Sample:
   <u>hostile</u> reaction
   - A friendly
   - B mean
   - C startled
   - D crazy

1 <u>rural</u> area
   - A country
   - B farming
   - C urban
   - D coastal

2 pulled <u>taut</u>
   - A loose
   - B tight
   - C free
   - D down

3 <u>drab</u> appearance
   - A pale
   - B boring
   - C happy
   - D bright

4 <u>lush</u> surroundings
   - A barren
   - B luxurious
   - C rainy
   - D normal

5 <u>vague</u> answer
   - A whispered
   - B wrong
   - C specific
   - D careful

6 <u>insert</u> the key
   - A make
   - B turn
   - C put in
   - D take out

7 <u>descend</u> the mountain
   - A glimpse
   - B go down
   - C go up
   - D destroy

Reading Skills Practice Test 8
Reading Comprehension

Read each passage. Then, fill in the circle that best completes each sentence or answers each question.

SAMPLE

The hole in the ozone layer, a protective shield around our planet that blocks harmful sun rays, is bigger than ever. Ozone is a layer of gas in the stratosphere, a part of the atmosphere 7 to 31 miles above the Earth. Tests show that the hole over the South Pole is now about the size of North America. As the hole grows, there's more risk of getting severe sunburns, which can cause skin cancer.

1 According to the passage, what is one effect of the growing hole in the ozone?
Ⓐ There is more risk of being poisoned by the stratosphere.
Ⓑ There's more risk of getting severe sunburns.
Ⓒ It rains more on Earth.
Ⓓ It rains less on Earth.

A. The peanut butter and jelly sandwich is an everyday food for some kids. But for other kids, the sandwich can be a killer. That's because some kids are highly allergic to peanuts. In severe cases, even the presence of peanut particles in the air can cause a life-threatening allergic reaction.

An estimated 32 million people in the United States suffer from food allergies. Of these, about 5.6 million are kids. And of all the allergies kids can have, peanuts are among the most dangerous. That's why many schools have taken action.

Some schools just restrict the use of peanuts and peanut butter. Other schools have banned peanut products altogether. That means absolutely no peanut butter and jelly sandwiches allowed!

1 Why shouldn't some kids eat peanut butter and jelly sandwiches?
Ⓐ They don't like peanut butter and jelly.
Ⓑ Peanut butter and jelly is fattening.
Ⓒ They are allergic to peanut butter.
Ⓓ They are allergic to jelly.

2 What is the best title for this passage?
Ⓐ "Peanut Alert"
Ⓑ "A Great Sandwich Gone Bad"
Ⓒ "A History of Food"
Ⓓ "Peanuts Everywhere"

B. Many foster children move three or four times during their childhood years. When Aubyn Burnside learned that most of these kids had to use plastic garbage bags to move their **possessions** from place to place, she decided to do something.

From the age of 11, Aubyn, of Hickory, North Carolina, has been collecting suitcases for kids who must leave their homes. She wanted to give the children a little security and dignity with the suitcases.

Aubyn began her suitcase collecting by posting signs at libraries, grocery stores, churches, and schools, asking for donations. In less than a year, Aubyn provided suitcases for 300 foster children in her county. Today, Aubyn's volunteer program, Suitcases for Kids, provides luggage to foster children around the world.

1 In this passage, the word **possessions** means
Ⓐ clothes.
Ⓑ homework.
Ⓒ belongings.
Ⓓ brothers and sisters.

2 Which of these is an opinion?
Ⓐ Aubyn provided suitcases for 300 foster children in her county.
Ⓑ Many foster children are forced to move three or four times.
Ⓒ Suitcases give foster children a little security and dignity.
Ⓓ Suitcases for Kids provides luggage to foster children around the world.

C. For years, the biggest airplane flying was Boeing's 747. In 2004, the Airbus Company built an even bigger aircraft. The A380, a double-decker plane, became known as a super-jumbo. That's because it was even bigger than other jumbo jets, like the 747, at the time.

The new superplane is a virtual city in the air. The A380 can fly more than 550 people from coast to coast. The plane is so big that it can contain cafes, sleeping rooms, and even a gym. Just imagine exercising 30,000 feet in the air!

Not everyone is convinced that super jumbos like the A380 are such a good idea. Critics say that passengers may not like being on such a big plane. The huge number of passengers can create all kinds of difficulties. How long, for example, does it take for so many passengers to get on board? And will airports need new designs to handle lots of these monster flying machines?

1 What is the best title for this passage?
Ⓐ "Superplane!"
Ⓑ "A History of Flying"
Ⓒ "Exercising in the Air"
Ⓓ "Airports"

2 How is the A380 different from the 747?
Ⓐ It is bigger.
Ⓑ It is smaller.
Ⓒ It doesn't carry passengers.
Ⓓ It doesn't use airports.

D. Miles below the ocean's surface, **hydrothermal** vents spit out water hot enough to melt lead—650 degrees. These vents provide energy for tube worms, clams, and octopuses that live in the deepest depths of the sea. The water from the vents contains chemicals that change into food for hundreds of deep-sea species.

Although oceans cover more than 70 percent of Earth, the deep sea remains largely unexplored. But scientists are making new discoveries every year. In 2020, scientists photographed a large shark that glows in the dark. The kitefin shark uses this ability to disguise itself from predators.

And scientists continue to seek out giant squids. Few giant squids have been seen alive, but several dead ones have washed ashore. A giant squid's remains can stretch for 60 feet. Its eyes are as big as hubcaps.

1 In this passage, the word **hydrothermal** means
(A) cold water.
(B) hot water.
(C) giant.
(D) tiny.

2 What is the main idea of this passage?
(A) Interesting things live at the bottom of our oceans.
(B) The giant squid is an incredible creature.
(C) Scientists don't really want to explore the oceans' depths.
(D) It's always incredibly cold at the bottom of the ocean.

E. Puerto Rico's El Yunque rain forest is the only rainforest in the U.S. national forest system. That's one reason to visit it. A better reason is that it's very beautiful.

More than 240 kinds of trees and 1,000 kinds of plants live in El Yunque. It also is home to over 60 kinds of birds. What makes it such a great home for these living things? It has a lot of water. El Yunque receives over 200 inches of rain each year. Plus, six major rivers trace their sources here.

Besides plants and animals, what else is there to see in El Yunque? There are several spectacular waterfalls, including La Coca Falls and La Mina Falls. And then there is the mountain of El Yunque itself. This mountain rises over 3,500 feet above sea level.

According to legend, El Yunque was the home of Yukiyú, the Taino Indians' protecting spirit. Tainos were the original inhabitants of Puerto Rico.

1 What makes El Yunque a great home for living things?
(A) It has a big mountain.
(B) It's in a great location.
(C) It has a lot of water.
(D) It's very cold all year-round.

2 The purpose of this passage is to
(A) describe the island of Puerto Rico.
(B) explain how rain forests work.
(C) persuade you to visit El Yunque.
(D) tell the history of the Taino Indians.

Vocabulary

Synonyms

Read the underlined word in each phrase. Mark the word below it that has the same (or close to the same) meaning.

Sample:

feeling <u>drowsy</u>
- Ⓐ awake
- Ⓑ sleepy
- Ⓒ unhappy
- Ⓓ excited

1 <u>fabulous</u> clothes
- Ⓐ great
- Ⓑ awful
- Ⓒ new
- Ⓓ old

2 <u>needless</u> waste
- Ⓐ enormous
- Ⓑ little
- Ⓒ unnecessary
- Ⓓ necessary

3 <u>swivel</u> quickly
- Ⓐ leave
- Ⓑ swim
- Ⓒ turn
- Ⓓ talk

4 <u>primary</u> problem
- Ⓐ main
- Ⓑ last
- Ⓒ other
- Ⓓ small

5 <u>wage</u> war
- Ⓐ pay
- Ⓑ make
- Ⓒ win
- Ⓓ lose

6 <u>bestow</u> a gift
- Ⓐ give
- Ⓑ take
- Ⓒ tow
- Ⓓ allow

7 <u>evident</u> problem
- Ⓐ unlikely
- Ⓑ obvious
- Ⓒ unclear
- Ⓓ unavoidable

Antonyms

Read the underlined word in each phrase. Mark the word below it that means the opposite or nearly the opposite.

Sample:

<u>exotic</u> fruit
- Ⓐ tasty
- Ⓑ sour
- Ⓒ ordinary
- Ⓓ popular

1 <u>panicky</u> feeling
- Ⓐ calm
- Ⓑ nervous
- Ⓒ good
- Ⓓ bad

2 <u>merciless</u> enemy
- Ⓐ evil
- Ⓑ mean
- Ⓒ compassionate
- Ⓓ helpful

3 <u>formal</u> dinner
- Ⓐ casual
- Ⓑ unplanned
- Ⓒ deluxe
- Ⓓ expensive

4 <u>teeming</u> hallways
- Ⓐ decorated
- Ⓑ empty
- Ⓒ filled
- Ⓓ overrun

5 <u>relish</u> the food
- Ⓐ love
- Ⓑ dislike
- Ⓒ swallow
- Ⓓ spit out

6 <u>wary</u> movement
- Ⓐ carefree
- Ⓑ cautious
- Ⓒ timid
- Ⓓ quick

7 <u>inferior</u> brand
- Ⓐ exterior
- Ⓑ popular
- Ⓒ superior
- Ⓓ expensive

Name _____ Date _____

Reading Skills Practice Test 9
Reading Comprehension

Read each passage. Then, fill in the circle that best completes each sentence or answers each question.

SAMPLE

Americans love to roller-skate. Millions of people in the United States enjoy this fun sport. But did you know that roller-skating has been around for more than 200 years?

It began in 1760. Belgian inventor Joseph Merlin was the first person to put on roller skates. Like many new skaters, he had trouble controlling them. After putting the skates on, he **inadvertently** rolled into an expensive mirror. Some things never change!

1 What is the best title for this passage?
Ⓐ "Skating Mishaps"
Ⓑ "Merlin the Magician"
Ⓒ "Ice-Skating History"
Ⓓ "The First Roller Skater"

2 In this passage, the word **inadvertently** means
Ⓐ purposefully.   Ⓒ quickly.
Ⓑ accidentally.   Ⓓ slowly.

A.   All dogs, from dachshunds to dalmatians, could trace their family tree to one common ancestor—the gray wolf.

How did wolves become dogs? Humans chose wolves with certain traits—like size, shape, color, and gentleness—and then bred them with other wolves. For instance, small wolves that were bred with other small wolves would produce more small wolves. Over thousands of years, this kind of special breeding developed different kinds of dogs.

So, the next time some little pooch comes strolling down the sidewalk, give it a little respect. That doggie has some pretty tough ancestors!

1 How did wolves become small dogs?
Ⓐ They mutated into dogs.
Ⓑ Humans bred them in certain ways.
Ⓒ They attacked the dogs and took their place.
Ⓓ They shrank from lack of food.

2 What is the purpose of this passage?
Ⓐ to inform you about how dogs share a common ancestor
Ⓑ to persuade you that dogs are great
Ⓒ to entertain you with small-dog stories
Ⓓ to scare you away from small dogs

B. One day a bunch of boys in Monahans, Texas, were playing basketball when a meteorite, or space rock, landed just 10 feet from where they were shooting hoops.

The meteorite was a brown, 2-pound, 11-ounce, foot-shaped rock. The boys soon learned that it was a stony meteorite.

Meteorites formed billions of years ago. Usually, they burn up completely as they fall toward Earth and are called meteors. When a meteor doesn't burn up completely, it falls to Earth as a meteorite.

The mayor of Monahans thought the meteorite belonged to the town, not the boys. The boys disagreed. They wanted to sell the meteorite and use the money for college. The Monahans city council sided with the boys. The boys eventually sold the meteorite to a rock collector for $23,000.

1 Which of these is the boys' problem?
Ⓐ The mayor thought the meteorite belonged to the town.
Ⓑ The city council sided with the boys.
Ⓒ The boys sold the rock for $23,000.
Ⓓ Their basketball game got interrupted.

2 What is the difference between a meteorite and a meteor?
Ⓐ Meteorites are meteors that do not burn up completely.
Ⓑ Meteorites are smaller meteors.
Ⓒ Meteors are small and meteorites are large.
Ⓓ Meteors are round and meteorites are foot-shaped.

C. In Atlanta, Georgia, hundreds of thousands of items are locked behind a steel door that isn't meant to be opened for 6,000 years.

The door fronts an airtight, watertight room that was once an indoor swimming pool. The room is filled with record albums, books, dolls, newspapers, watches, and recordings of old radio broadcasts.

Why fill a room with such treasures, then seal it for centuries? It's because the room is a time capsule. Its purpose is to send a message to the people of the future.

A time capsule is a container filled with objects that represent a particular part of life at a particular time. The Atlanta time capsule is called the Crypt of Civilization. It was sealed in 1940. Its creators chose items that would show all the achievements of human civilization, from the beginning of time through the 1930s.

1 When was the Crypt of Civilization sealed?
Ⓐ 1930   Ⓒ 1950
Ⓑ 1940   Ⓓ 1960

2 Why would people want to make a time capsule?
Ⓐ They want to get rich.
Ⓑ They want to keep special items safe from harm.
Ⓒ They want to become famous.
Ⓓ They want people in the future to know about their lives and accomplishments.

D.   The words to the United States' national anthem were written by Francis Scott Key. He wrote them during the War of 1812.

Key had a good friend who was taken prisoner by the British during the War of 1812. Key was very worried about his friend. So he went to the British ship where his friend was being held prisoner.

The British agreed to let his friend go. There was just one catch. The British were about to attack Baltimore. They would have to wait on the ship during the attack.

It was a terrible battle. The sky turned black with smoke. Key kept his eyes on an enormous American flag hanging over Baltimore's fort. As long as that flag was raised, American troops were surviving.

When the battle was over, the flag was still hanging! Key was so overcome, he jotted down the words that would become the United States' national anthem.

1 Why did Key go to the British ship?
Ⓐ He wanted to write a song.
Ⓑ He wanted to help his friend.
Ⓒ He wanted to spy on the British.
Ⓓ He wanted to help the British.

2 After the battle, what effect did the sight of the American flag have on Key?
Ⓐ It caused him to cry for joy.
Ⓑ It caused him to write the words to the American national anthem.
Ⓒ It caused him to hug his friend and the British soldiers.
Ⓓ It caused him to become angry and set off bombs.

E.   Bryan and Curtis were just sitting down at the computer when Javier came running in. He looked upset.

"I've lost my new scarf that my mom knitted for me! I can't believe it. I've looked everywhere. What am I going to do?"

"Calm down," Curtis said. "The best thing to do is to stop and think about where you might have left it."

"I already told you, I've looked everywhere," Javier cried.

"Are you sure? Maybe you forgot about some place you went. Tell us everything you've done this afternoon."

"Well, first I went by Coach Corran's office to ask about tomorrow's game. Then I rode my bike to the store to pick up some things for my mom. And then I came here to your house."

"Are you positive that's everywhere?"

"Yeah, I think so. Oh, wait a minute. After the store I stopped off at the deli to grab a snack. Oh, wow, I remember now. I left my scarf there!"

1 What did Javier do after he stopped by Coach Corran's office?
Ⓐ He went home.
Ⓑ He went to the store.
Ⓒ He went to the deli.
Ⓓ He went to Curtis's house.

2 Which of these adjectives best describes Javier?
Ⓐ bashful   Ⓒ calm
Ⓑ forgetful   Ⓓ fierce

Vocabulary

Which Word Is Missing?

In each of the following sentences, a word is missing. First, read each sentence. Then choose the missing word from the list beneath the sentence. Fill in the circle next to the word that is missing.

Sample:

As they waited for their big surprise, the children were _____ with excitement.

Ⓐ unhappy   Ⓒ breathless

Ⓑ bored   Ⓓ agonizing

1 Lisa's arms were bare, and she _____ in the cold.

Ⓐ trembled   Ⓒ sweated

Ⓑ screamed   Ⓓ argued

2 If Joey hadn't forgotten his house key, he wouldn't be in this _____.

Ⓐ adventure   Ⓒ excitement

Ⓑ voyage   Ⓓ predicament

3 The new action movie coming out next week is hotly _____.

Ⓐ criticized   Ⓒ unbelievable

Ⓑ anticipated   Ⓓ disgruntled

4 He was a good worker with an _____ job record.

Ⓐ extreme   Ⓒ atrocious

Ⓑ unblemished   Ⓓ outlandish

5 Worried about his sister's wound, John shouted with _____, "I have to see the doctor now!"

Ⓐ fervor   Ⓒ ennui

Ⓑ malice   Ⓓ tact

6 That was quite a _____ the scandal caused.

Ⓐ tirade   Ⓒ quest

Ⓑ triumph   Ⓓ sensation

7 The accused waited for the trial to start with some _____.

Ⓐ boredom   Ⓒ trepidation

Ⓑ glee   Ⓓ recreation

8 The thief _____ took all of her money and valuables.

Ⓐ genially   Ⓒ ruthlessly

Ⓑ gleefully   Ⓓ accidentally

9 She couldn't believe that the thief could be such a _____.

Ⓐ gentleman   Ⓒ personage

Ⓑ villain   Ⓓ savior

10 He's so _____, he would probably talk to an empty room.

Ⓐ reticent   Ⓒ fiendish

Ⓑ verbose   Ⓓ benevolent

11 True chocolate lovers will not leave even a _____ of chocolate cake on their plates.

Ⓐ morsel   Ⓒ mortal

Ⓑ meager   Ⓓ variety

Reading Skills Practice Test 10
Reading Comprehension

Read each passage. Then, fill in the circle that best completes each sentence or answers each question.

SAMPLE

If you have a sweet tooth, you might have strong teeth. Researchers in Japan recently discovered that chocolate might help **prevent** cavities. They say the outer shell of the cocoa bean, the main ingredient in chocolate, fights tooth decay. One day soon, you could brush your teeth with chocolate toothpaste. However, until experts are sure, trading in toothpaste for a chocolate bar isn't such a sweet idea.

1 The best title for this passage is
Ⓐ "Could Chocolate Prevent Cavities?"
Ⓑ "Sweets in Japan."
Ⓒ "New Ways to Brush Your Teeth."
Ⓓ "The Cocoa Bean."

2 In this passage, the word **prevent** means
Ⓐ aerate.
Ⓑ stop.
Ⓒ deepen.
Ⓓ make.

A. During winter, some people feel unhappy and have trouble concentrating.

Doctors call these winter **blues** SAD, or Seasonal Affective Disorder. Scientists believe people get SAD because there is less daylight in winter than in other seasons.

This lack of light can affect the body. To help people with SAD, doctors find ways for them to get more light. For example, patients might sit in front of a light box or spend more time outside.

1 The main idea of this passage is
Ⓐ winter is dangerous.
Ⓑ less light makes some people feel sad.
Ⓒ people need to exercise.
Ⓓ all seasons are the same.

2 In this passage, the word **blues** means
Ⓐ sadness.   Ⓒ music.
Ⓑ colors.   Ⓓ winter.

3 Going outside helps people with SAD because
Ⓐ fresh air is good.
Ⓑ they need less light.
Ⓒ they need exercise.
Ⓓ they need more light.

B.   Did Martians once exist on our neighboring red planet? Researchers have discovered evidence that suggests lakes and oceans once covered Mars. And where there is water, there are often living things.

The Mars Global Surveyor, a spacecraft that mapped Mars, took pictures that show sedimentation, or layers of rock. These layers suggest lakes and oceans once existed on parts of Mars. If that's true, then Mars was probably a lot more like Earth in its early days than was **previously** thought.

Water and an atmosphere similar to Earth's would have given Mars the key ingredients for life. If life did once exist on Mars, there should be evidence in the form of fossils. To find the fossils, scientists will have to dig deep into the rock layers.

But even if there were Martians, they were probably tiny, and not the four-eyed green monsters you see in cartoons and comic books.

1 In this passage, the word **previously** means
   Ⓐ stupidly.   Ⓒ before.
   Ⓑ scientifically.   Ⓓ after.

2 In order to find evidence of life on Mars, scientists will have to
   Ⓐ dig deep into Mars's rock layers to look for fossils.
   Ⓑ do research on the Internet.
   Ⓒ avoid looking at cartoons or comic books.
   Ⓓ take new pictures with the Mars Global Surveyor.

C.   Playing and sledding after a snowstorm may be fun, but blizzards are serious business. Every year, people die when blizzards hit. But you can beat a blizzard's dangers by being prepared. Before a blizzard starts, you should:
   • Stock up on food and supplies. Don't forget batteries. Blizzards often knock the power out.
   • Help your parents get those snow shovels and snowblowers out!
   • Listen to the weather forecasts. Stay off the roads if a storm is about to hit.
Once a blizzard hits, if you do go outside remember to:
   • Dress in layers. This helps to keep you warm by trapping your body's heat.
   • Offer to help any elderly people you know by shoveling snow or getting supplies for them.
   • Go inside the second you feel numb or sleepy.

1 When should you stock up on supplies?
   Ⓐ before the blizzard
   Ⓑ during the blizzard
   Ⓒ after the blizzard
   Ⓓ never

2 Based on the passage, you can conclude that
   Ⓐ preparing for a blizzard isn't important.
   Ⓑ blizzards are more serious than regular snowstorms.
   Ⓒ blizzards are never deadly.
   Ⓓ blizzards only happen in the Arctic.

D. It happened during the 1998 Goodwill Games on Long Island, New York. Sang Lan, a gymnast from China and the Chinese national vaulting champion, was practicing the vault. Like a thousand times before, she **launched** her body into the air, but somehow, this time, she lost control. Hurtling forward, she crashed to the floor, head first.

The accident injured Sang's spinal cord, paralyzing her from the chest down. Confronted with such a life-changing event, Sang approached it the way she had gymnastics—by working hard. She began relearning life's basic skills. She had to learn simple actions all over again. Things that most of us never think about, like getting dressed or eating, were major tasks.

But Sang never looked back with anger or sorrow. Instead, she applied herself to her new goals: getting a college degree and becoming an advocate for the disabled. And in 2014, Sang also became a mother.

Says Sang, "When I had just gotten injured, I did think, 'What would I be doing if I hadn't got hurt?' But now I don't think about it. Regrets are pointless."

1 In this passage, the word **launched** means
- Ⓐ propelled.
- Ⓑ rolled.
- Ⓒ stepped.
- Ⓓ relaxed.

2 What was one of Sang's new goals in life?
- Ⓐ eating
- Ⓑ getting dressed
- Ⓒ getting a college degree
- Ⓓ going back to gymnastics

E. Baseball-card collecting may be all about Mike Trout and Fernando Tatís Jr. nowadays, but baseball greats like Mickey Mantle and Willie Mays were a big part of the trading-card craze many years ago.

A company called Topps began making the cards as a way to sell its bubble gum. The gum isn't included anymore, but the cards are still popular.

During the 1950s and '60s, children started tossing the cards into shoe boxes to save. Now some of those collections are worth thousands of dollars. The most wanted of the 2½-by-3½-inch trading cards are the "rookie cards," which are players' first cards. Cards that are autographed are also popular. Old cards can be worth a lot. In 2020, a 1952 Mickey Mantle card sold for $5.2 million.

1 Why did Topps start making baseball cards?
- Ⓐ people wanted to collect them
- Ⓑ children needed something to play with
- Ⓒ the company was trying to sell its bubble gum
- Ⓓ they knew they would be worth a lot of money

2 A good title for this passage would be
- Ⓐ "A Short History of Baseball Cards."
- Ⓑ "How to Sell Your Baseball Cards."
- Ⓒ "The Future of Baseball Cards."
- Ⓓ "The Story of Micky Mantle."

Vocabulary

Synonyms

Read the underlined word in each phrase. Mark the word below it that has the same (or close to the same) meaning.

Sample:

extreme <u>fatigue</u>
- Ⓐ tiredness
- Ⓒ fatness
- Ⓑ happiness
- Ⓓ beauty

1 <u>arduous</u> task
- Ⓐ easy
- Ⓒ lengthy
- Ⓑ difficult
- Ⓓ daily

2 always <u>quarreling</u>
- Ⓐ arguing
- Ⓒ talking
- Ⓑ moving
- Ⓓ singing

3 will you <u>surrender</u>
- Ⓐ come
- Ⓒ cry
- Ⓑ stay
- Ⓓ give up

4 use <u>caution</u>
- Ⓐ thinking
- Ⓒ protection
- Ⓑ carefulness
- Ⓓ help

5 <u>commend</u> his judgment
- Ⓐ criticize
- Ⓒ praise
- Ⓑ listen to
- Ⓓ accept

6 <u>appropriate</u> behavior
- Ⓐ mature
- Ⓒ proper
- Ⓑ immature
- Ⓓ wrong

7 <u>massive</u> stadium
- Ⓐ filled
- Ⓒ dark
- Ⓑ small
- Ⓓ huge

Antonyms

Read the underlined word in each phrase. Mark the word below it that means the opposite or nearly the opposite.

Sample:

<u>esteemed</u> mayor
- Ⓐ disrespected
- Ⓒ elected
- Ⓑ respected
- Ⓓ elderly

1 <u>bonded</u> together
- Ⓐ joined
- Ⓒ disconnected
- Ⓑ living
- Ⓓ walking

2 <u>remote</u> area
- Ⓐ lovely
- Ⓒ populated
- Ⓑ grassy
- Ⓓ televised

3 <u>purchase</u> clothing
- Ⓐ shop
- Ⓒ take
- Ⓑ carry
- Ⓓ sell

4 <u>meager</u> salary
- Ⓐ small
- Ⓒ new
- Ⓑ big
- Ⓓ professional

5 <u>exported</u> goods
- Ⓐ erupted
- Ⓒ brought in
- Ⓑ fancy
- Ⓓ sent

6 <u>unjustly</u> accused
- Ⓐ fairly
- Ⓒ nearly
- Ⓑ sadly
- Ⓓ personally

7 <u>stifle</u> a groan
- Ⓐ let out
- Ⓒ keep in
- Ⓑ try
- Ⓓ whine

Tested Skills	Item Numbers				
	Practice Test 1	Practice Test 2	Practice Test 3	Practice Test 4	Practice Test 5
Cite textual evidence to support analysis of what the text says explicitly as well as inferences drawn from the text.	B2, B3, C2, D1, E2	C1, C2, D1, E1	A2, D1, E3	A1, B2, B3, C1, E2	A1, D1, E2
Determine a theme or central idea of a text and how it is conveyed through particular details; provide a summary of the text distinct from personal opinions or judgments.	A2, B1, C1		B1, C1, D2	B1	C2
Describe how a particular story's or drama's plot unfolds in a series of episodes as well as how the characters respond or change as the plot moves toward a resolution.		E2	C2		B1
Determine the meaning of words and phrases as they are used in a text, including figurative and connotative meanings; analyze the impact of a specific word choice on meaning and tone.					
Analyze how a particular sentence, chapter, scene, or stanza fits into the overall structure of a text and contributes to the development of the theme, setting, or plot.	A3		A1, B3	A2, D2	B2, C1
Determine the meaning of words and phrases as they are used in a text, including figurative, connotative, and technical meanings.	A1, E1	B1, D2	E2	C2, D1, E1	E1,
Determine an author's point of view or purpose in a text and explain how it is conveyed in the text.	D2	A2, B2	A3, B2, E1	D3	A2, D2
Trace and evaluate the argument and specific claims in a text, distinguishing claims that are supported by reasons and evidence from claims that are not.		A1			
Use context as a clue to the meaning of a word or phrase.	Synonyms 1–7, Antonyms 1–7	Synonyms 1–7, Antonyms 1–7	Which Word is Missing? 1–7	Synonyms 1–7, Antonyms 1–7	Synonyms 1–7, Antonyms 1–7
Use common, grade-appropriate Greek or Latin affixes and roots as clues to the meaning of a word.			Which Word is Missing? 1–7		
Use the relationship between particular words to better understand each of the words.	Synonyms 1–7, Antonyms 1–7	Synonyms 1–7, Antonyms 1–7		Synonyms 1–7, Antonyms 1–7	Synonyms 1–7, Antonyms 1–7

© Scholastic Inc.

Scholastic Success With Reading Tests • Grade 6   45

Tested Skills	Item Numbers				
	Practice Test 6	Practice Test 7	Practice Test 8	Practice Test 9	Practice Test 10
Cite textual evidence to support analysis of what the text says explicitly as well as inferences drawn from the text.	A2, B1, D1, D3	A1, D1, E3	C2, E1	A1, B2, C1, D1	D2, E1
Determine a theme or central idea of a text and how it is conveyed through particular details; provide a summary of the text distinct from personal opinions or judgments.		B1, C1	A2, C1, D2		A1, C2, E2
Describe how a particular story's or drama's plot unfolds in a series of episodes as well as how the characters respond or change as the plot moves toward a resolution.		A2		B1, E2	A3
Determine the meaning of words and phrases as they are used in a text, including figurative and connotative meanings; analyze the impact of a specific word choice on meaning and tone.	C2	B2	D1		
Analyze how a particular sentence, chapter, scene, or stanza fits into the overall structure of a text and contributes to the development of the theme, setting, or plot.	A3, C1	B3, C2, E1	A1	D2, E1	B2, C1
Determine the meaning of words and phrases as they are used in a text, including figurative, connotative, and technical meanings.	A1, D2	E2	B1		A2, B1, D1
Determine an author's point of view or purpose in a text and explain how it is conveyed in the text.	B2	C3, D2	B2, E2	A2	
Trace and evaluate the argument and specific claims in a text, distinguishing claims that are supported by reasons and evidence from claims that are not.	C3, E2	A3, D3	C2	C2	
Use context as a clue to the meaning of a word or phrase.	Synonyms 1–7, Antonyms 1–7	Synonyms 1–7, Antonyms 1–7	Synonyms 1–7, Antonyms 1–7	Which Word is Missing? 1–11	Synonyms 1–7, Antonyms 1–7
Use common, grade-appropriate Greek or Latin affixes and roots as clues to the meaning of a word.				Which Word is Missing? 1–11	
Use the relationship between particular words to better understand each of the words.	Synonyms 1–7, Antonyms 1–7	Synonyms 1–7, Antonyms 1–7	Synonyms 1–7, Antonyms 1–7		Synonyms 1–7, Antonyms 1–7